Gentlemen – Protect yourself from
Vampires in Divorce

SAIANAND RAMAN

To be Forewarned is to be Forearmed

Table of Contents

How will this book protect you in the Divorce Battle surrounded by Vampires?

There are two ways of learning to protect yourself with regard to divorce. One is learning 'What To Do' which majority opts for. The other way which serves most effectively in divorce battle is learning, 'What Not To Do'. This book will protect you by creating awareness on What Not To Do. By highlighting the undesirable consequences victims faced by doing things they shouldn't have done, due to ignorance. It Forewarns you thereby Forearming you.

Another common reason for ignorance is lack of time, and lack of readily available precise information. With this book, what you need to do is, invest the least of your valuable time to safeguard you from lifetime regret.

This book will empower you to have total control and command over your so called 'Super Lawyers', by prohibiting them from intimidating, pressurizing, blackmailing, threatening you. And also makes you aware about malpractices lawyers indulge in collusion with opposition lawyer.

On the whole, this book will definitely give you the confidence to take the vampires head-on and emerge victorious without losing your peace of mind.

There are so many things you need to know about the way your gladiator approaches your case, most of which your gladiator can't tell you. He or she would rather you not hear them, knows you don't want to hear them, and may not even be aware of them, so you don't hear them. If your gladiator were totally truthful, though, you might read something like this. I certainly don't mean to imply that all gladiators have all the characteristics reflected here, but enough of them are present enough of the time that it makes sense for you to be sensitive to them. To read a different perspective, see the note at the end.

Dear client:

I am pleased that you have hired me to represent you in your divorce. I'm pleased because I need the money you and others like you pay me. I'm tired of working with people like you who are always fighting and never happy, and often unhappy with me, but I feel trapped now and don't know how I could change my practice at this point in my career without a huge financial setback, so I hang on and do the best job I can, the best way I know, for clients like you.

If you're like most people going through divorce, you've heard a chorus of voices -- from your mother to your neighbor to the person who cuts your hair -- warning that you better get a mean "junkyard dog" lawyer. I don't like being a junkyard dog lawyer, and I don't think it would be in your best interest for me to be, but I have to give you the impression early on that I am so you will hire me. I don't like doing it, but you demand it, so I do it.

That means that when we met in our first consultation, I talked about how experienced I am. I gave you an optimistic assessment of what you would give up and what you would get working with me. If your spouse had come the same day instead of you and presented the very same facts, I would have given your spouse an equally optimistic assessment from <u>their</u> perspective. I learned long ago not to lose any sleep about doing this. You demand it, and I'm going to give it to you so you will hire me.

You can see what happened now, can't you? I gave you an optimistic assessment of your case from your perspective, and then one of my colleagues gave your spouse an optimistic assessment of the case from your spouse's perspective. Together, we worked knowingly or unknowingly to convince both of you that the other is being unreasonable and that you each needed us to win you a better deal.

I told you in our initial consultation that you should avoid communicating directly with your spouse about anything other than parenting of your children. I did this because nothing is so important to me as client control. I want to be the gatekeeper of all communications between you and your spouse, so I can decide how much information to provide to you and what "spin" to put on it. This will make you and your spouse more suspicious of each other, and it will make you more dependent on me. I like that, at least in the early stages of divorce negotiations.

I required you to pay a large retainer when you hired me. I told you that I have a fixed retainer for all divorce clients, or I may have told you that I set your retainer after carefully considering the complexity of your case, the time I expect to put in, and the risk that my estimates might be too low. In reality, though, my technique for setting your retainer was far simpler: I charged the highest retainer I thought I could get. The reason I did this is that the retainer is often the only money I ever see for representing someone in a divorce case. I may try to bill you and get paid later, but many of my clients don't pay me anything after the initial retainer, even though they owe me a great deal of money, and I hesitate to sue them for fear they will counterclaim for malpractice and drive up my insurance premiums. The fact that I have so much trouble getting clients like you to pay me what they owe me is another reason my work is so unpleasant for me.

I also will work to appear successful. I may drive a luxury car and maintain a sumptuous office, because I want you and my colleagues -- especially my colleagues -- to believe that I am earning lots of money. In one sense, I _am_ earning lots of money. I charge a high hourly rate, and I have a great deal of business, so I have high billings. I also have a high overhead, however, and I have trouble getting paid. In reality, I have financial struggles just like you do.

There's more than a 93% chance that your case will settle before trial. Nevertheless, I will prepare your case as if you were going to trial. This will be wasteful and expensive. I will conduct lengthy discovery, including interrogatories, requests for the production of documents, and depositions, charging you a great deal of money to prepare documents that I simply have printed from my word processor with minor changes.

I will do this not because it's in your best interest but because I'm afraid of being embarrassed in front of other lawyers and judges and because I'm afraid you will sue me. The result is that you and/or your spouse will spend a great deal of money preparing for a trial we know will almost certainly not occur. I've heard that much of this could be avoided by simply exchanging documents and affidavits, but that's not what I'm used to doing. If there's a better way, I don't know it, and even if I knew it, I probably wouldn't do it. The way I practice law is what I know and understand, and it's safe for me.

I live my professional life in and around the courthouse. I gauge my schedule and my priorities to make sure cases that have an imminent court date are ready to present. This means that if your case <u>doesn't</u> have an imminent court date, it will be hard to get me to focus much attention on it. Your case will move much more slowly than you would like.

When we are at the courthouse, there will be huge blocks of time when I will leave you alone while I negotiate or just swap stories with your spouse's lawyer. Every now and then, I'll report back to you on progress and tell you how negotiations are going. You probably will find it jarring that I'm so friendly with your spouse's lawyer. Remember, you and I have a temporary relationship. Your spouse's lawyer and I have seen each other several times a week for years and our relationship will continue long after you're gone from my life. It's not surprising, then, that I'm more attentive to that relationship than I am to the one with you.

Early on in our relationship, you are in emotional distress, you believe that no one in the world has ever faced the problems you are facing, and you view me as a savior who can protect you from all the cruel insults you are facing. Over time, however, you will begin to stabilize emotionally, you will begin to view me and my services more realistically, and you will begin to realize just how expensive all this is becoming. You may begin to resent me, and you may place a lower priority on paying my fee. You will also begin to hold me accountable for producing results that I know are unrealistic.

Although at the outset I stated an optimistic assessment of your case, over the term of our relationship I will become increasingly pessimistic with you about your chances. I will do this because, by then, I will become tired of you and tired of your case. I will want you to become more flexible in negotiations so I can reach an agreement with your spouse and your spouse's lawyer. By then, I will have spent enough time on your case to justify keeping the entire retainer, and I will be afraid that I may never see any more money, so I will press you to reach agreement with your spouse.

Also, as our relationship continues, I will be increasingly harder to reach. I may fail to return your phone calls, or I may call you back but be evasive about giving you useful information, always seeming in a hurry. I will do this perhaps without even realizing I'm doing so, primarily because it will be unpleasant for me to deal with you when you become increasingly unhappy.

Often an agreement will happen because you and your spouse meet over the kitchen table or on the phone and work it out, and then communicate it to your respective lawyers. This agreement may be remarkably similar to what the two of you could have agreed had you been willing to cooperate with each other at the beginning through mediation or negotiations, but you won't think about that by then, because to do so would be to admit to yourself that you've wasted several thousand dollars on legal fees. Even though I told you at the outset not to talk to your spouse, I will by then be secretly glad that you did and will work to help your agreement succeed (if I can avoid spending much time on it). Remember, by then, I will want out.

I have learned that most of my business comes by referral from other professionals, so it's more important to me that referral sources feel good about me than those clients feel good about me. I devote lots of attention to my relationships with judges, other lawyers, and other professionals. On the other hand, I have over the years become quite comfortable with unhappy clients, even clients who complain about me to the bar association. This bothered me in my early years of practice, but I've become jaded to it now. The bar association knows as I do that clients of divorce lawyers are often unhappy. I know the bar association is accustomed to receiving these complaints and taking them with several grains of salt, so it doesn't worry me much that you might complain about me.

I like you, and I'm a caring professional who wants to do a good job for you. I've learned not to trust you, though. I wish I <u>could</u> trust you, but I've been burned too many times by clients like you. I'm going to keep my guard up. Now that you know the way this works, let's get started.

Yours Sincerely

Your Divorce Lawyer

Legal fees are a cost of doing business. While the Web has made it easy to do some of the very mundane work on your own (say, filing for incorporation or ginning up a bare-bones operating contract), do-it-yourself lawyering has huge limitations.

The trick is finding and hiring the best, most trustworthy professional help for the buck. I'm going to help you.

First, **start with your inner circle**: friends, neighbors and colleagues. This initial search may not turn up any attorneys with the specific expertise you need, but don't despair. While your sister's divorce lawyer may not be much help when it comes to selling your business, he may know a few attorneys perfect for the job. Lawyers know other lawyers–use them for recommendations.

Don't want people to know you need legal help? You can **hunt on the sly** by contacting local bar associations. They have lists of attorneys. Beware, though: The bar association hasn't blessed those

11

attorneys, beyond perhaps assuring they are licensed to practice and have not been disbarred. Further due diligence is still required.

Next step: **Hit the Web**. To be fair, there are still a few accurate rating systems for lawyers. One useful online resource is martindale.com, which rates lawyers on a scale of A, B and C. Those ratings are done by other lawyers and are fairly reliable. Martindale also offers additional information on attorneys, but be aware that the attorneys themselves prepare those write-ups. Lawyers.com and findlaw.com can help too, but understand that attorneys pay to be listed there.

Once you assemble a short list, remember that **size matters**. Law firms range in size from one lawyer to over 3,000. If you are Gordon Gekko and want to do a hostile takeover of Bluestar, think big firm. If you are looking for someone to negotiate a lease for your new office, a small shop will be able to handle that as well, if not better. (After all, you don't want a marquee firm letting its younger, more inexperienced staffers learn on your dime.) Remember that letters to legal opponents from big shops tend to carry more weight.

Next step: At this point you're ready to set up an initial consultation. But before you pick up the phone, do even more homework. Check each attorney's Web site. Does it look cheap or professional? Is there a lot of sizzle but little substance? Next, **check their track records**—as in how they fared in specific decisions. While subscriptions services, such as Westlaw, Lexis or PACER, are happy to sell you this information, your local law library can probably get it for a lot less.

At your first meeting, be ready to **ask a lot of questions** regarding both your particular matter and the lawyer's practice. Some good ones: How many similar matters have you handled? What were the results of those cases? Which lawyer in the firm will be working on your case? Will there be any limitations on the scope of the representation? How will you be kept informed about the progress of the case? How quickly do you respond to phone calls and e-mails?

How can I reach you after normal business hours?

The lawyer may charge you for the initial consultation. Don't take this as an affront. Many potential clients use these get-to-know-you sessions to get free legal advice. (If you owned a grocery store, you wouldn't let someone try a brand of paper towels to see how they work and then, maybe, pay for them.) If the attorney does charge, simply ask if the amount will be credited to the bill later on.

Which brings me to fees, whatever you do, **understand precisely how you will be charged—** this will save you all sorts of headaches later on.

Lawyers generally charge one of three ways: by the hour, a one-time flat fee or by contingency (percentage of the amounts recovered). Not every fee structure is permitted for every legal situation. For personal injury cases, most lawyers charge a contingency fee; for certain business transactions (such as incorporation), they'll charge a flat fee; and for most other matters, they will ring up by the hour.

Hourly rates can range from $100 to $1,000. (Generally speaking, you get what you pay for.) Bear in mind, too, that an attorney who charges $200 per hour may take twice as long to do the same thing as an attorney who charges $300 per hour.

There are additional questions you should ask, depending on the type of fee structure. Example: If the engagement is on an hourly fee basis, you will want to know (1) the hourly rate, (2) the minimum billing increments, (3) whether there is a charge for every phone call, letter and e-mail, (4) an estimate of the number of hours the case will take (I find this question very difficult to answer), (5) what expenses might be required and (6) what happens if the case takes longer than anticipated. (Many of those same questions are relevant in flat-fee agreements too.)

If yours is contingency arrangement, you will want to know (1) the likelihood of recovery (remember, there are no guarantees in the law), (2) an estimate of the recovery (same warning), (3) the percentage being charged, (4) the percentage most lawyers charge for the same type of case, (5) anticipated expenses and (6) what happens if the case settles immediately.

Get a handle on all of that and you'll be ready to **ink an engagement letter**. This is your working contract between you and your attorney, so read it carefully. The engagement letter should describe the nature of your legal matter, as well as all of the terms and conditions of the relationship, including the hourly rate, the minimum billable increment (you should always insist on being billed in six-minute increments, not 15), the expenses you will be responsible for, the amount of the retainer and any other matters you agreed to.

If you are unsure about something in the engagement letter, call and ask. Otherwise, if you sign and return the letter, you will be bound by it.

The work doesn't end after you ink that contract, of course. Ask your lawyer to provide you with copies of everything that goes out relating to your case (the cost of the copies will most likely be passed on to you). I find that providing too much information is better than not providing enough.

Think your attorney missed his calling as a golf caddy? Fire him. After all, you control the relationship.

If you owe money, your lawyer may insist on being paid before turning over your file to you or his replacement—whether or not he can actually make those demands is determined by the ethics laws in your state. (The state bar association can field that and related questions.) And don't think you are at a disadvantage because lawyers run the bar associations—attorneys do a good job of policing themselves.

When you do hire a divorce attorney, it's more than a matter of running your fingers through the lawyer ads in the yellow pages until you spot the word "divorce" or simply hiring the lawyer who helped you negotiate your office lease or draw up your will.

- You need to hire an attorney experienced in family law.

In some states, attorneys can be *board-certified* in family law. These lawyers specialize in divorce cases and other kinds of family law issues. To be certified, they must have significant trial experience and pass a rigorous test. To maintain their certification, they must receive substantial continuing education in family law each year, generally twice the amount of required continuing education of non-board certified family law attorneys. This type of family law attorney tends to charge more and demand higher retainers to begin a family law case than those who are not board-certified, but they are usually more experienced.

- The attorney you hire should talk to you in plain English, not legalese.

- The attorney should be someone you trust and feel comfortable with, because you may have to reveal highly personal information about yourself and your marriage.

- If you have young children, look for an attorney who makes it clear that during your divorce you must put your children's needs first and that he or she will not pursue unreasonable demands for child support or help you pursue vindictive child custody and visitation arrangements.

- And last, but certainly not least, your lawyer should be affordable.

Appropriate skills and experience

An old adage states, "There are horses for courses." This saying is as true for an attorney as for any other professional. In other words, when you select a family law attorney, you want one with the legal skills and knowledge needed to get the job done for you:

- If you need help negotiating your divorce agreement, the ideal attorney is a problem solver, works well with people, is adept at compromise, and is comfortable in court. Although you and your spouse may have no intention of going to court, an attorney's trial record and history of success in court can have some bearing on his or her ability to negotiate a settlement with your spouse's attorney.

- If you know from the start that you're headed for a divorce trial, you want an attorney who has considerable courtroom experience. Not all lawyers do.

- It is also helpful if the attorney you choose is familiar with the family law judges in your jurisdiction. Knowing the courtroom style of the judge who's likely to hear your case and how the judge has ruled on previous cases similar to yours helps your attorney adapt his or her legal strategy and style to that particular judge.

Don't base your hiring decision on which attorney has the nicest office. A fancy office in an expensive building says nothing about the adequacy of a lawyer's legal skills. At the same time, don't assume that just because you pay a lot of money to an attorney that his or her legal representation is appropriate to your needs or is of high quality. Also, don't let a lawyer's physical appearance influence your hiring decision.

If your financial situation is complex, the lawyer you hire should either have a solid understanding of the issues and laws that pertain to your divorce or work closely with other lawyers or financial experts who have that knowledge, such as a CPA or appraiser. Remember, negotiating your divorce agreement is as much about financial matters as it is about ending your marriage.

Personal style

If you are relying on an attorney to do more than simply review your divorce paperwork, you must be prepared to share details about your personal life, marriage, and finances. Therefore, you must feel comfortable with whoever represents you.

In addition, your attorney should share and support your basic philosophy or attitude toward your divorce. For example, if you want to keep things as calm, cooperative, and nonadversarial as possible, then avoid attorneys who like to "go for the jugular."

Do not confuse your attorney with your therapist or religious advisor. Your attorney's clock is usually running regardless of whether you call with a legal question or to complain about your spouse.

Affordability

If you don't have much money to spend on legal help, you may have to hire a relatively inexperienced lawyer instead of a seasoned professional. New attorneys tend to cost less than lawyers who have been practicing law for years and already have solid reputations. However, working with an up-and-coming or novice attorney has a potential advantage. In order to build up a good reputation, the attorney may be willing to work a little harder for you than a seasoned lawyer would.

Most family law attorneys bill for their services on an *hourly basis.* Few agree to take a *flat fee* based on the total amount of time and labor they think your divorce requires. Estimating up-front just how much time is necessary to finalize your divorce is difficult, because no lawyer knows exactly how any divorce is going to play out.

You're more apt to find an attorney who'll take your case for a flat fee if your divorce is 100 percent amicable and if the tasks the attorney will perform are very well defined. You may be able to find an attorney willing to accept a flat fee if your legal needs are very specific and very limited — for example, you just need some paperwork filled out and filed.

Among other things, an attorney's hourly rate depends on your region of the country and whether your community is rural or urban. Those of you living on the East and West Coasts can expect to pay the most.

Depending on where you live, on average the services of a divorce attorney will cost you anywhere from $100 an hour to more than $600 an hour, *plus* expenses.

Do stay involved:

When you hire your lawyer, don't simply hand control of your life over to him or her and walk away. Your divorce is critical to you, and it's too important to be delegated away and ignored. Stay abreast of developments on a daily basis. Find a lawyer who wants you to be as involved as you do. Two things to look for in a lawyer who wants to keep clients involved: same day delivery to you of all documents that come in or go out of the lawyer's office (email is a great option for this) and 24/7 access to your case file. **Ideally, your file will be available on an extranet on your lawyer's website.** If you can access your credit card and bank statements online, your divorce file should be online, on your lawyer's website, as well. Many lawyers use technology to make your life less stressful and more convenient; find one who uses the latest technology to help you stay involved. Involved clients are able to maintain control, reduce anxiety and make better judgments about their future, which helps them to reach positive outcomes in their divorce.

Do educate yourself:

Knowledge can be your greatest ally. Research the divorce laws of your state, whether through a local law library or the internet. RosenDivorce.com is the most comprehensive divorce website in North Carolina. The site features a discussion forum with questions answered by lawyers, a child support calculator, the latest cases from the North Carolina Courts, numerous essays and information on all divorce issues, seminar videos, and lots more. Reading the information on this site will dramatically improve your effectiveness and efficiency in interacting with your lawyer and negotiating with your spouse.

Don't hire a mediator without getting legal advice first:

Often, people think that hiring a mediator is a good move, in trying to resolve their divorce. The critical mistake these people are making is this: mediators cannot give legal advice. Their role is only to help people agree; the drawback is that they may help you agree to something that you would not have agreed to if you had sought legal

25

advice first. Timing is everything here:
you should never, ever hire a mediator without
first obtaining legal advice from a lawyer whose
only role is to represent your best interests. In
fact, any good mediator will insist that you go and
get legal advice before any agreement is reached,
anyway. If you choose to mediate your dispute,
get the legal advice before you begin mediation. It
is more efficient and safer.

For example, if one spouse is hiding assets or
income, and refuses to come clean, you may have
to head to court where a judge can order your
spouse to comply. Or, if one spouse is unwilling to
compromise, mediation probably won't work.

Don't assume your lawyer will take care of everything.

For many of us in our generation, getting taken care of was the norm. So when divorce strikes, our first inclination is to put our fate in the hands of a white knight, another protector, our lawyer. Yes, you need a lawyer, but before you even walk into that lawyer's office, you must educate yourself about divorce law in general and your state's laws in particular. Get on the Internet or buy a book and start researching. If you're not fully educated and proactive, you will wind up with a settlement you'll regret for the rest of your life.

Be More Pro-Active:

Ask questions of your divorce lawyer, be very inquisitive about communication between the courts and your lawyer. Ask for all copies of anything filed with the courts before they are filed.

Don't Be a Victim of Divorce Lawyers Dirty Tricks

If there is any inflammatory language being used in documents sent to the courts or the opposing counsel you will be able to have it removed. Being an active part of the divorce process will help the steps you go through during divorce move along at a faster rate.

You are Responsible for Your Divorce Lawyer:

You are responsible for your lawyer's actions. Don't be intimidated by his / her law degree. They know the legalities of the situation but you know yourself and your spouse. Insist that the attorney follows your instructions as far as keeping the conflict to minimum.

Who Decides?

When considering a settlement, lawyers need to examine if the settlement is actually in the client's best interest. Many times, a side offers settlement terms which don't fully compensate the other side's injuries and damages. However, lawyers seeking a quick finality to the case may pressure the client to accept it. The decision whether to settle or not belongs to the client.

If your ex or ex's lawyer keeps **delaying the divorce** then this can be a dirty divorce trick as well. Basically every motion that can be filed will be filed in a case such as this to delay the divorce for as long as possible. If your ex knows you are financially strapped then this tactic can be very useful as it will run up your legal bills and force you to take a settlement.

The opposite of this is to **rush to a quick financial settlement** as fast as possible. When such an event occurs in your case then you should be wary of what your ex could be hiding from you. Typically there are assets that are hidden in the divorce and by settling the case quickly these assets never become known and hence protected from you.

What can I do if I felt pressured to sign the agreement?

A Victim's Experience: My attorney didn't notify me about the court date until two days before, and it was obvious that he wasn't prepared for it. he didn't call for any witnesses to the mental abuse I had suffered, although several people including a therapist had sent in affidavits and said they were willing to testify. After literally all day of negotiating, I agreed to a settlement that I was not ok with under much duress. On top of this, my attorney set it in stone by questioning me ON THE RECORD to say I was in the right frame of mind to agree to the terms set forth. I wanted to scream NO! But I agreed. Is there anything I can do about this now?

Expert's Answer: If you agreed to it, there isn't much you can do now. I hear this kind of thing a lot. To others reading this, I would urge that you not agree to anything unless you are sure. Don't let your attorney talk you into it. It's hard to stand up for yourself, but you have to because no one else is going to do so. I think it is also very common to agree to something, think it is the right decision and then regret it later.

Do divorce attorneys use negotiating tricks?

Yes. Not all of them, but a lot of them. After all, they went to law school, they are attorneys, and they want to get the best deal for their client in any (legal) way they can.

Many attorneys who use "positional bargaining" tactics use various "tricks" to try to get their way. The problem is, if the other attorney has some negotiating skill and savvy, these tricks do not work very well.

For example, a well-known ploy is the "one more thing" trick. Imagine that you and your attorney have been in intense negotiations with your spouse and your spouse's attorney for several hours. You've finally hammered out what appears to be a reasonable agreement. As you are just about ready to close the deal, your spouse's attorney says "Oh, we want one more thing."

That "one more thing" can be anything. It could be that your spouse wants "a little more" parenting time. It could be that he or she wants "a little more" money for alimony or child support. It could be that he or she wants the brand new 80 inch plasma TV that you just purchased with your bonus.

In extreme cases, I have seen attorneys and their clients renege on signing a Marital Termination Agreement after it has been fully written up, and even though it accurately reflects the terms of the agreement that the parties reached in mediation. The other side wants "one more thing." This kind of comportment can be considered to be unethical, and it certainly shows bad faith, but that does not stop attorneys from engaging in it.

Your spouse's attorney knows that you have just spent a lot of time and effort to get to an agreement. The attorney knows that you have a lot invested in the negotiating process. The attorney knows that you have an emotional interest in getting done with the divorce and avoiding trial. The attorney believes that, instead of looking at the total balance sheet with the "one more thing" added and realizing that it is now unfair, you will just say "okay, I give up–take one more thing."

You do not have to say this. You can evaluate the "one more thing" and decide how important that issue is to you. Usually it's important to you and your spouse knows this, which is why it was held up as "one more thing," for her to grab at the end of the negotiations. If your attorney is experienced, he or she will have held something in reserve. Often, this is not so much the "one more thing" that you want as it is the possibility of proceeding with the process if negotiations fail. Or, your attorney will know how to say "No" in a way that communicates to your spouse that if he or she insists on getting "one more thing" it will end up costing her more than it is worth.

WHY MEN LOSE IN FAMILY COURT?

You are looking for answers to a specific family law problem. Let me assure you that you've come to the right place. We have the answers you need!

The subject of this article is "Why Do Men Lose In Family Court?" I have spent the last 23 years attempting to answer this question. After considerable research, case evaluations and client interviews I believe I now have the answer.

Twenty three years ago I went through a brutal divorce. Actually, at the time of divorce we were very friendly with one another and agreed to settle out of court. My Ex-wife, through a paralegal filed for divorce and like most men I simply agreed to the terms. I walked away with nothing! I surrendered the house, *($40,000.00 in equity)* the boat, the car, furniture etc. etc...Everything I had acquired in 13 years of marriage was suddenly gone. We had three children and I wanted them to have the benefit of these items. Although I didn't realize it at the time I could have and should have made better agreements that would have benefited all members of my family in a much greater way. Looking back I simply didn't know what a good agreement was or how to make the deal. I was so concerned about maintaining a good relationship with my ex that I avoided anything that might have resulted in a legal battle. I should have filed my response with the court and requested an equitable division of property, custody, visitation and a support order that was based on my Real income. In general I should have been more attentive to the legal issues. This was truly a mistake!

Like most men I had adopted the common belief that men always lose in divorce proceedings so why not just surrender everything now and avoid the inevitable. What I didn't realize at the time was that I wasn't doing anyone any favors by surrendering everything to my ex-wife. Ignorantly giving up my property caused my wife to develop a false confidence in the legal system that would soon allow her to sue me again and again and again. Like many women she understood the prevailing thought of men that they always lose in family court and she capitalized on this belief. Therefore it didn't matter any longer how much I had given to her the fact that I didn't know what I was doing was extremely obvious. Despite everything I had surrendered, ignorantly failing to make fair and equitable agreements at the time of my departure from the family home was a colossal mistake and was a personal invitation for her to sue me later. I would in time realize that money and property are no substitute for a well-written, fair and equitable agreement of ALL issues. Like the American Express advertisement declares "Don't leave home without it!"

I had also surrendered a number of other rights simply because I was ignorant and wasn't aware of the significance of these rights. Mainly rights to my children. I had mistakenly believed that women always get custody of children and Dads always get the standard every other weekend visitation schedule. In fact I was so ignorant I actually thought this was the law! Little did I realize that even after I had given everything I had, I would still have to give more.

About 2 years later I acquired a new love interest and our "friendly divorce" turned into a legal nightmare! She went to an attorney and was advised to take me back to court to increase child support, decrease visitation, contempt of court and a host of other issues. Not knowing any better I went to an attorney, paid a $3500.00 retainer fee and went to court. It was my belief that we had fairly resolved all of our legal issues in the beginning and I really didn't understand why she wanted more or how she could get more.

After 3 court hearings and an additional $3000.00 in attorney fees *(total $6,500.00)* later I had gotten my butt kicked! My attorney did absolutely nothing! He was worthless but certainly richer. On the way home from the courthouse I realized how unfair the family law system of justice was for men and began a search for answers. Further, I realized that just having an attorney does not mean there will be a successful resolution. A few days later I saw a newspaper advertisement for a Fathers Rights support group near my home. It sounded interesting so I decided to attend one of their meetings.

The following Friday I arrived at the meeting discouraged and without hope. As I walked to my seat I passed a number of tables with pamphlets and books and other written materials all directed at men with family law problems. Most of these materials were advocating political reform of the family law system. I grabbed one of everything!

Once in my seat the meeting began with a number of men sharing their stories of severe prejudice and bias in the family court. The first thing I realized was that I was not alone in what I had experienced in and out of court. After two or three testimonies a gentleman went to the podium and addressed the crowd. The subject of his speech was "Why men lose in Family Court."

The gentleman opened his speech with these questions: "How many of you came here tonight because you are currently in a family law case and are looking for answers?" Everyone in the room raised their hands. "How many of you defaulted by not responding to divorce or hearing papers?" Many raised their hands. "How many of you are struggling to pay your child support?" Again almost everyone raised their hands. "How many of you are being harassed by the District Attorney *(Child Support Enforcement)* for child support?" "How many of you have had their driver's licenses suspended or taxes taken due to unpaid child support?" Many raised their hands. "How many of you only see your kids every other weekend?" About half the room raised a hand. "How many of you paid large amount of money to an attorney to resolve your problems and still lost the battle?" Again almost everyone raised their hands. Finally he asked, "How many of you are happy with the outcome of your case?" The room suddenly became quiet and no one raised their hands.

When the speaker had finished asking the questions it was very apparent that most of the men in the room, including me, didn't know the first thing about avoiding or resolving a family law problem! It was a moment of realization that we had each failed due to our own ignorance. These men, myself included were like lambs headed to slaughter. None of us had a clue as to what we had done wrong or how we could still resolve our own legal problems! What a pathetic group of men! This wasn't what any of us expected.

The speaker continued by explaining why men lose in family court. "Yes there is bias, prejudice and discrimination in family court towards men. Yes the family court system is broken and needs reform. However, despite these problems most of you have failed because you didn't take the time to learn how the system works." As he spoke he gave numerous examples of mistakes that men make. *(These Mistakes are discussed in the Fathers Rights Survival Guide.)* "Men lose in family court because they simply don't do their homework and women do!"

Most men, myself included, believe they are capable of resolving just about any problem. Most have run businesses, negotiated purchases of homes and/or cars and have been successful resolving other large problems at work and home. Consistent with their success in other areas of their life, when their long-term relationship's end they believe they can "cut a deal" or somehow avoid a problematic legal case without making legally filed agreements. Call it male machismo or pride but in reality it's called arrogance! Failing to learn how the family law system works will doom your case. Like one leading motivational speaker has stated: "Failing to plan is planning to fail!" There is no substitute for correct information and knowledge.

The speaker closed the meeting with this exhortation: "I want each of you to make a commitment. A commitment to your friends, family, to your children and to yourself! I want you to commit to learning how the family law system works. I want you to commit to changing the outcome of your case! This week I want each of you to go to a law library or bookstore in your area and read anything and everything you can on family law. Once you have acquired the needed knowledge set a goal, form a plan and don't give up until you get what you want and need!"

As I drove home from the meeting I was filled with mixed emotions about what the speaker had said. On one hand I was encouraged that I could take control of my case, learn how the system works and resolve my ongoing legal problems. On the other hand I was very discouraged when I realized I had caused my own legal problems. I had lost in court because I had failed to learn the "rules of the game." Like millions of other men I thought I could strike an easy out of court settlement and go on with my life. How wrong I was! This was a very hard lesson for me! I was a college graduate. I was fairly intelligent and should have known better. My Ex-wife wasn't to blame, I was! I did this too myself! My failure was her victory!

The very next morning I decided to make the commitment to resolve my legal problems. As the speaker instructed I went to the local law library and read numerous books and articles. The following day I went to numerous bookstores and read many self-help books on family law. In addition, I searched the Internet and read everything I could about divorce and Family Law.

The more I read the more I realized how mistaken I had been.

Over the next six months I continued studying family law and attending the meetings sponsored by the Coalition of Parent Support. The Fathers Rights movement and my own personal knowledge began to flourish. In fact, I eventually became a board member of the statewide group. After a few months, I even enrolled in paralegal classes at a community college. A year later I was so committed that I enrolled in law school. Boy what a turnaround!

My first year of law school I did two important things. I started my own organization called Fathers Rights, Inc. I began offering self-help legal assistance and counseling to men. Also, I returned to court to resolve unfinished legal business. This time I was prepared for battle! I had done my homework!

On the day of court I discovered that my ex-wife had retained the same attorney she had used previously. When he saw me in the hallway I am sure he thought this would be quick and easy. After all I was so misinformed the first time. The attorney approached me and began telling me how ridiculous my request for hearing was and that he was going to "stick it to me" if I didn't drop the matter immediately. With confidence, I informed him I would not do so and would see him before the Judge. We did discuss the legal issues at hand and you could see that his attitude towards me was much different than before. The attorney made his routine offer of settlement that I promptly refused. He was now very concerned. He had recognized that something was very different.

About an hour later, we ended up in front of the Judge. Here's what happened: My child support went from $1,113.00 per month plus health insurance of $225.00 to $243.00 a month in child support and she paid the health insurance. Further, my visitation time-share with my kids went from 5% to 43%. It turns out that my ex-wife was earning over $100,000.00 a year. I had filed subpoenas with her bank and employers based on a rumor I had heard that she had a second job but I wasn't sure. The subpoenas revealed that she did in fact have a second job. She had not revealed this to the court. Even her attorney was unaware of this! In fact her "second job" earned her significantly more money than her regular job. Big mistake on her part! Needless to say I won the relief that I was seeking! My ex-wife may have won a previous battle but ultimately lost the war. Over the next six months there were other legal issues that I was able to resolve. I stopped her from moving out of state with the kids. In fact this did not even require a hearing. She accepted my legal explanation of what the court would in fact do and she decided not to move.

On another occasion the principal of the school that my children attended felt she had no obligation to provide me with copies of my children's report cards and other information. *(Emergency medical contact information, Notice of parent-teacher conferences, transcripts etc. etc...)* It's significant to note that my ex-wife's mother was the vice-president of the school board. The principal, vice-principal, teachers and school nurse were aware of this. No doubt that the decision to deny my parental rights was directly related to my mother-in-laws powerful position. Well, I filed a suit in civil court naming the principal, vice-principal, school nurse, the entire local and county school boards, and the California board of education.

At the hearing the County's attorney spoke with me and expressed regret that this matter had to be filed. He agreed that the schools position could not be legally supported based on the family code. He informed them that their position was in error and the policy of preventing a parent with joint legal custody from viewing his children's school records was illegal and should be instantly changed. The matter was settled in the hallway and never made it to the Judge and for good reason.

Here is the best part of this story: After successfully resolving the legal issues my ex-wife "got the message." She realized that I would never again allow myself to be used as a legal punching bag. There would be no more rolling over. No more defaults, no more passivity. I had become a pro-active participant. I had finally learned how the system worked and would vigorously defend myself in any future issue that might arise. And guess what? Once she understood she could no longer win automatically, Lo and behold we never had another legal dispute! Immediately following the last court hearing our conversations became civil but solely limited to the lives of the kids. Exactly the way it should be! *(And should have been from the beginning)*

WHY MEN LOSE IN FAMILY COURT?

My children are grown now and my personal family law struggles are over. I learned the hard way that what you do now will determine the quality of the relationship you will have with your children in the future. People forget that children are only in the custody of either parent for a relatively short time. After they reach the age of majority is when the real relationship begins! I was fortunate in that I discovered my failure in time. I was able to reverse a never-ending trend of court hearing after court hearing with no end in sight. It all changed that one evening after the meeting when I decided to commit to making needed changes in my attitude and approach to my case. I had learned a valuable lesson. Know the rules before you play the game! Once I discovered the rules of the game it all changed.

Now let me ask you! Why have you picked this book? Are you looking for answers to your family law problems? Are you the Parent, Grandparent, girlfriend, sister or new wife of a man having problems in family court? Are you confused? Lost? Frustrated? Angry? Let me give you the same advice I was given years ago. Your case *(or the case of the person for whom you are concerned)* will never be resolved until you *(they)* take the time to learn how the family law system works. That is Laws, case laws just those related to their specific case. You need not read the entire divorce law of your state, to write law exam, that's for legal professionals. You just search and read those parts of law specific to your case. Unless you are Bill Gates and have thousands and thousands of dollars to spend on attorney's fees you need to learn how Family Law works. **You can be sure your Ex has!** In fact, if you don't take the time to learn how the family law system works no attorney or other legal professional can ever help you! Now I'm not suggesting that you need to take paralegal classes or go to law school as I have done. But you must commit to learning the simple steps you can take now to resolve your present legal issues and avoid additional issues in the future.

Have you ever seen the movie "Monsters Inc."?

It's a cute animated Disney film about Big Scary Monsters. All day long they go through magical doors, each leading into a bedroom of a young child sleeping at night, and the monster's job is to scare the shit out of that kid and extract screams for money.

That's very much like the life of a lawyer. He goes about his work day, new situations come up, he gets involved and scares some people, he gets paid. The better he is at scaring people, the better paid he is. I'm not attacking lawyers for doing their job, everyone's got to eat and earn a living. I just want to show you how best to deal with him.

You have to understand this fundamentally: When someone hires a lawyer to threaten you, he's not hiring someone to figure out the legal matters involved, he's hiring someone to threaten you. Crushing you and making you bend is the first priority, the law is just a tool.

In earlier times, when a dispute arose you would hire some muscle, or even a hit man to take care of it. In civil society we hire attorneys. They are the modern day muscle men. Unfortunately the law is often unjust or unclear and attorneys are

48

therefore able to exact injustice, sometimes terrible injustice, on behalf of their clients.

"I learned long ago, never to wrestle with a pig. You both get dirty, but the pig likes it." George Bernard Shaw

THE APPROACH: After a busy day scaring people, when a monster enters your bedroom to scare you, you need to scare HIM. He should open the door, step inside, and then you close the door, lock it, terrify the living shit out of him until the monster begs you to let him out.

A threatening attorney must be made to realize that his life is much better returned to intimidating average people. He should want nothing to do with you. You are the pig who enjoys getting dirty. When your name is mentioned to him, it should trigger a recurring nightmare and sudden stomach pain.

That's my approach anyway. And it's worked well for me. Back in the glory days of my career as a Commercial Real Estate Broker, I would receive a very threatening attorney letter at least once a month, but often about once a week. They are like toilet paper to me, the words on the paper didn't concern me.

That's because involving attorneys is such a common negotiating practice when dollar values rise and several million dollars are at stake. The attorney letter is always written to sound as terrifying as possible; threatening enormous amounts of money, threatening life as we know it, threatening to sue everyone and everyone's grandmother.

The more threatening the letter, the more references to precedent case numbers, the more terrifying the tone, the more they're covering up. The more they are compensating for lack of a legitimate case. Learn to smell a bluff.

What I do next depends on the attorney's tone on the phone when I call him. I've noticed 3 types.

It's true, and it is rare, sometimes you call a lawyer and his tone is actually warm and a little friendly. That's good. He might actually be a reasonable guy and might try to make a fair situation out of this. Go ahead and work it out fairly. Getting an attorney involved is a hostile act, but see if there's still an opportunity to resolve the matter cooperatively.

Usually his tone is cold and technical. That's just fine. I usually cut right to the chase and tell him "the letter I received is without any merit whatsoever. You've given us 1 month to send your client $350,000 before you file a lawsuit. That's nice of you, but let's not drags this out and create movie suspense. Go ahead and file the suit tomorrow if that's in your client's best interest. But if I receive any more communication from your office beyond that this matter is dropped, I will sue your client and sue you personally for malicious prosecution. Surprisingly, often enough that got the attorney to drop the matter.

Remember, attorneys do not want legal problems resolved. Resolution of conflicts dries up his billable hours. He wants as much chaos and destruction as possible. That way he becomes more important.

However, it's amazing how despite a tolerance for causing pain for others, he will usually have a very low tolerance for pain himself. Most attorneys have no balls. They aren't businessmen and they're usually unwilling to take even the slightest personal risk. Attorneys are very uncomfortable about being attacked personally, and they're not used to it. You have a lot of leverage over them by going after their license and their reputation, two things they guard dearly. They just won't risk anything important on a bluff.

I've even had attorneys hang up on me mid-sentence realizing it's not worth their time speaking with me for another second, let alone pursuing further nonsense legal action. That is a good outcome.

The third type of encounter is when, often enough, the tone of the attorney picking up the phone is rude, nasty, and extremely condescending. I'm not going to deny it, I get a certain sense of excitement when I hear this. My blood starts rushing and I can't hold back my smile. This situation now merits my favorite legal response.

I tell him "We're going to keep this short and sweet. Do you have a pen and paper? I don't want to send back any letters or emails, I want you to write down my formal response. Are you ready? Good. The formal response to your client is, 'Eat Shit and Go Fuck Yourself'. Did you get all that, or should I repeat it?" That should catch him off guard. Always, he'll quickly ask me why I'm behaving so unprofessionally. I don't tell him to please look in the mirror when he asks these things, I just tell him to "Be a good professional and pass along the message. Goodbye."

That is a powerful approach for so many more reasons than you can quickly realize.

In a fight you want to limit your opponent's moves and force him in the direction you want him to go. The other side is now forced to carefully consider their options, their options have just been drastically limited.

I make sure I don't seem like I'm crazy and emotional, I seem crazy and deliberate. No one wants to get into a legal fight with someone who's crazy and deliberate.

Also the nasty rude condescending attitude usually comes from the big fish lawyers that charge $500 to $900 an hour. His client went through pains to find the worst expensive weapon to fire at me. Someone really wants me scared. The attorney just received a fat retainer and must justify his cost. After all that puffery and bravado, he really really doesn't want to have nothing to show for himself but to relay a message to eat shit and go fuck yourself.

He has a reputation to uphold among his profession and beyond. Everyone knows him as a big shot. He does not like to doubt himself. His wife, children and friends ask him how things are going. No one speaks to the king of the jungle like that! But what can he do about it? Someone paid him a lot of money to scare me and I'm not scared.

The big shots are usually more sensitive. They may dress expensively, speak eloquently, be well educated, but make no mistake, they are not that sophisticated, they are savages. The way I deal with them is I think about how to deal with a 3 year old throwing a temper tantrum for attention. If he behaves, I've got a cookie for him. Otherwise he's going to enjoy some discipline.

The point is that I make it very clear that I'm completely uncooperative when anyone tries to strong arm me with bullshit. I'll usually demonstrate that clearly by doing something that will not look good in front of a judge. Because IT WILL NEVER GET IN FRONT OF A JUDGE. As I said earlier, most legal cases are without much merit. The bible is interpreted in a million different ways, and unfortunately our legal code is even more widely interpreted. Attorneys need your cooperation to intimidate you with the law. If you're not cooperative, there's no way the other side will take a questionable business dispute all the way to court, spending a couple hundred thousand dollars doing so, with a very shaky chance of winning. It's not a smart business move, and ultimately there is a businessman paying and authorizing the attorney's actions. So when an attorney gets hostile with me, I remain very uncooperative and demonstrate that clearly by doing things that could look terrible in front of a judge.

Let me be clear, I would never tell a moderately reasonable attorney to "eat shit and go fuck yourself". I tell that to the hardcore condescending assholes. I've done it many times. It has NEVER defused the situation. They always get pissed and riled up. That's fine with me because they were already uncooperative and hostile to begin with. This is not a bluff technique, I'm making it clear that being a dick is not a productive way to deal with me. And since, in my experience, their cases have always been vague or based on bullshit, their ONLY options left after that are to pursue trial on a weak case, or become friendlier.

Side Note

My approach assumes the other side has something to lose personally and won't find it in their interest to pursue legal action against me at any cost. I can imagine this approach wouldn't work at all with a government agency run by bureaucrats spending taxpayer dollars. Even if their case is weak and trivial nonsense, they go all the way, and they appeal if they lose. Also young attorneys looking for experience can often be stupid and reckless and willing to ruin everyone's life by pushing cases forward on their client's dime that shouldn't move forward. The same fundamental principles apply, but it can call for different approaches outside the focus of this article, which may include discrediting the young attorney in the eyes of his client, causing his client to fear representation from him, and bypassing the young attorney altogether.

Also this article refers to attorneys I've encountered in the business world and has nothing to do with attorneys who help plan estates, engage in criminal law, etc. I'm only talking about dealing with attorneys threatening you, not about dealing with attorneys you may hire to defend you.

Quick tip: When you do engage the other side (or their lawyer), whatever you do, never say the line "I'm taking this all the way to trial, I don't care what this costs me". Everyone says that. That doesn't work with someone like me. I smell blood. "Oh really, you don't care what this costs you? Alright then, let's find out how much you really don't care." People who say they don't care about the costs often cave sooner, because they are showing that they're weak. They're showing that they really don't have much solid to fight you with except their loudly stated tolerance for pain. That tolerance is easy to test. And it's usually very low when there's not much else but puffery to back it up. Any modestly wise person cares about the financial effects of litigation. Don't try to pretend you're stupid, or else you're going to look stupid.

A much better approach if you want to demonstrate you're unconcerned about a lawsuit is to find a creative reason why you might actually enjoy a lawsuit. Maybe tell the attorney something like this, "While no one enjoys a grueling court case that wastes everyone's time, energy and money; now that I think about it I would be really excited for the opportunity to depose your client. He has acted in bad faith and illegally on a number of matters that I personally resent and I simply cannot wait to hear how he will answer for himself under oath. Do me a favor and tell your client to file the lawsuit and let's take this all the way to court. I think this will be very interesting."

There's more to this than I can describe in this article, but you get the idea. I'm not advocating bluffing, I'm advocating standing up for yourself. That's what this article is about. Ultimately you're dealing with a hostile situation that probably won't be able to be resolved cooperatively anymore. A legal fight, like any other kind of fight, requires that you take some risks or else the other side will have all the leverage and will wipe the floor with you. Once someone is attacking you and you're in a fight, you either grow some balls, or you bend over.

Attorneys are hated because they're in a great position. They get to attack you with no repercussions. In fact the more fighting there is, the more they benefit. You will need to get creative to gain leverage and find their pressure points. Attorneys are smart to intimidate people into settling large amounts of money over absolute bullshit. Because too often it works. Most people who work hard to build their life and savings are too confused and afraid of the law to adequately fight back and defend themselves.

If you have clearly done someone wrong, then you deserve to pay for it. I'm not writing this to help assholes. This advice shouldn't help much if the other side has a legitimate claim against you for clear injustice. This is about standing up to legal intimidation as a negotiating tool. From my experience that is what most legal action has been about. If you've ripped people off and they're suing you, I hope you get fucked, and I fully support the lawyer that will help do the fucking.

Truth is I don't totally consider the attorney the bad guy. Someone hired him to wreak havoc and terror to get his way. The attorney is just doing what he's paid to do. It is the attorney's client that is pursuing justice or injustice.

Attorneys have gone through extra years of school at considerable expense, and endured grueling hours to pay their dues. They want to get paid for it. They don't usually care if they damage or ruin your life unjustly.

That's why people need to know how to stand up to them.

The higher you rise and the better you do in business, the more legal challenges you will encounter. You'll be surprised at the reasons people invent to take from you, gain leverage against you, or just harass you.

Many good friends of mine are lawyers and I've had a lot of experience with a wide assortment in the business world. I can safely say that few people have less respect for the law than lawyers. Abuse of law is not just common, it defines the industry.

Don't let them push you around.

If you're willing to look a monster in the eyes, you just might find that he has no teeth.

I am not in favor of dirty tricks during divorce. However, pretending they never happen doesn't do anyone any good, either.

Divorcing men need to understand the full range of tactics some wives use, and they need to be proactive —not reactive —as they work to secure the best possible divorce settlement. To that end, if you are contemplating divorce, you need to know about a tactic I see quite often in financially complex divorce cases:

Many wives will also indulge in,

Stall and delay. By repeatedly rescheduling court hearings and/or filing excessive motions and requests for evidence, a wife can drive up his husband's legal costs and stretch out the time during which he must take care of his job responsibilities. In these cases, the wife is hoping he'll run out of money and be forced to agree to her settlement offer, which is often extremely unfavorable to him.

Exert pressure to proceed too quickly.

21 Signs That Your wife May Be Hiding Marital Assets during Your Divorce

A wife who wants his husband to agree to a "quick" settlement may have something to hide. For instance, very early in the process, the wife's attorney may send over a settlement proposal for the husband to review and counter. Usually, this means the wife just wants to get the divorce over and done with quickly, and she wants her husband to settle for what appears to be a reasonable offer. The problem, of course, is that in many cases, he has not received all the discovery (Bank) documents requested, so he doesn't have complete knowledge about key financial matters, such as marital assets, income sources, expenses, what they owe and what's owed them.

Rushing to get a settlement is especially sneaky if the wife has been busy hiding assets and/or income and now she is trying to get him to agree to an unfair settlement proposal.

Deny access to financial resources.

Unfortunately, many husbands do not take a hands-on approach to the family finances. During a divorce, a wife can use his lack of knowledge to her advantage.

Red flags seem obvious, once you know what to look for. You may have good reason to be suspicious if your wife:

• Maintains complete control of bank account information and online passwords.

• Is secretive about financial affairs.

• Owns a P.O. box or private mail drop box, which receives account statements and bills.

• Has meaningful unreimbursed business account expenses.

• Deletes one or more personal financial programs, Quicken or Quickbooks.

• Says the computer containing important financial records has mysteriously "crashed." Then, she removes the hard drive for a data retrieval attempt, and it's never to be seen again.

• Acts pushy when obtaining signatures on important documents, like tax returns and deeds.

"I need to get this to our accountant today," she insists.

• Proposes an execution of mutual durable power of attorneys for "estate planning" purposes.

• Enjoys out-of-town business junkets with his befriended, slippery financial advisor.

• Develops SIDS (Sudden Income Deficit Syndrome). "My business is failing" suddenly crops up.

• Suffers an income decrease without a corresponding reduction of expenses.

• Binges on unusual purchases of flashy items, such as a car and jewelry.

• Reports a dramatic decrease in value of marital and/or business investments.

• Owns multiple cell phones or numbers over a relatively short period of time.

21 Signs That Your wife May Be Hiding Marital Assets during Your Divorce

• Makes frequent trips to countries with relaxed banking laws.

• Exhibits childish greed and claims of entitlement.

• Makes unusual purchases of toys or art that could be sold later.

• Starts drawing on large amounts of debt.

• Is involved in drug abuse.

• Gambles more frequently than usual and is placing money "on account" with casinos.

• Opens multiple business or personal bank accounts without obvious reasons for having that many.

A wife who hides assets usually has very specific, predictable objectives. In general terms, his goals are to:

1. Hide, understate, or undervalue certain assets,

2. Overstate debts,

3. Report lower than actual revenue, and/or

4. Report higher than actual expenses.

Most tactics are predictable, **too**. Here are a few of the most predictable strategies along with the advantages and disadvantages for each:

• **Hoarding unrecorded cash**. *Advantage:* Removing cash (currency) lacks a paper trail, and

offshore bank accounts are relatively easy (from a legal standpoint) to open. *Disadvantage:* Laundering over $100,000 in currency can be time consuming and will likely require travel. Depending on the circumstances, this tactic could involve the very serious criminal acts of money laundering, violation of cash transfer reporting requirements, federal income tax fraud and perjury.

• **Secreting already recorded cash receipts.** *Advantage:* This can be completed as part of a complex accounting scheme, which may be too

complicated or expensive to discover.
Disadvantage: Once cash is recorded, its absence
or transfer is discoverable.

• **Understating revenue.** *Advantage:* The business
owner has lots of options from which to choose.
Some are simple and easy. Deferring revenue by
manipulating the timing of revenue or accounts
receivable may not constitute tax fraud.
Disadvantage: Depending on the business owner's
sophistication, this can require a fairly predictable
co-conspirator. If the co-conspirator is placed
under oath, the scheme could result in perjury
charges.

**Scams to hide money often involve handing cash
or transferring ownership of valuable assets to
buddies, siblings, or parents to hold until
sometime after the divorce is final.** These
schemes usually include deceptive cover stories,
financial statement manipulation and lying under
oath. Sometimes the stories even become more
intricate, involving failing businesses, gambling
addictions and other personal failures.

"The more believable the story is that the money is gone, the more likely the victim will give up looking for it,"

Timing is critical to detect schemes using financial statement manipulation, and benchmarks are key. Ideally, a husband must be financially aware and involved from the onset of his marriage. Consistent participation from the start is critically important because: 1) If your wife has been hiding income/assets over years or decades, it will become virtually impossible to trace/find them, and 2) Being financially aware and involved helps form the foundation of happy marriages where a divorce is not even a possibility.

Remember, your wife doesn't have to be a billionaire to be guilty of hiding assets. Dirty tricks happen more often than men expect, and you'll need to _**Think Financially, Not Emotionally**_® so you can keep your finances intact during the divorce proceedings while you plan for a secure financial future post-divorce, as well.

The biggest mistake divorcing spouses can make is being in the dark about finances. If your spouse has always handled all of the financial decisions in your household and you don't have any information about you and your spouse's income and assets, your spouse will have an unfair advantage over you when it comes time to settle the financial issues in your divorce.

If you suspect your spouse is planning a divorce, get as much information as you can now. Make copies of important financial records such as account statements (eg., savings, brokerage, and retirement) and all other data that relates to your marital lifestyle (eg., checking accounts, charge card statements, tax returns).

If you believe your spouse may liquidate (sell or transfer to cash) assets or retitle marital assets without your consent, notify the holder of the asset or property in writing and get a restraining order from the court. Watch out for any cash held in joint checking and brokerage accounts, and the cash value of life insurance policies. If your spouse uses or moves assets without your knowledge, you may have to hire legal and forensic accounting experts to help you locate and value the assets.

Division of Property:

She has to pay half the debt, right?

Most jurisdictions apply a rule called "equitable distribution" or "equitable division" to divide assets and debt. The rule sounds an awful lot like "equal" division, and, sometimes, it is.

For example, retirement accounts (usually, the husband's) that accrued during the marriage are divided equally between ex-spouses. However, the same is not true for debt.

"Equitable" really means, do what is fair, and, for debt, that usually means the spouse who earns more pays more.

Do not go racking up a credit card bill with the assumption that your wife will be responsible for one-half the balance. If she earns less than you, she won't.

I received the inheritance. Not us.

If you receive an inheritance, the best thing to do is to title the property in your name only, deposit the money into an account bearing your name only, and do nothing but leave it alone – until you are safely divorced.

Why?

Because even though the inheritance is in your name and came from your parents, if you commingle it with marital property then your wife may have a claim to it.

Did you use the inheritance during the marriage to remodel the marital home? Did you put it in a joint bank account? If so, then that inheritance is not all yours – it's your wife's, too.

I'll keep the bank account, she gets the retirement.

A bank account and a retirement account may have the same balance on paper, but that does not mean they have the same value.

72

In the pursuit of a quick settlement with liquid assets, and hoping to avoid an expert's fees, some guys will swap a bank account for a retirement account.

The problem is $50,000 in the bank now is not the same as $50,000 in a retirement account now.

For one thing, to the extent you can access the retirement account, usually you must pay penalties and taxes for making a withdrawal. For another, there may be hidden costs, such as a loan in repay-status, tied to that account.

On the other hand, a future stream of income usually has more present day value than cash.

It's worth a meeting with a CPA or other specialist to have those accounts valued.

She can have the stuff in the house.

The household furnishings and holiday decorations may seem insignificant to you, but agreeing to give your wife "all the home contents" or "whatever she wants out of the house" is like writing a blank check – for thousands of dollars.

Think about it. The computers, televisions, china, entertainment systems, books, etc., all have a value. And that value really adds up.

Don't be afraid to have your home contents appraised so the value is taken into account in your overall property division. Otherwise, the divorce court is likely to assign no value or a nominal value to those contents.

Obtain the appraisal before you make the argument to your wife's attorney or in court, though. Most judges, and even some attorneys, will dismiss an argument that all of that stuff has value until they have an appraisal in hand.

I gave her the house so she's responsible for the mortgage.

Your wife might want the house, and she might be able to afford it, but awarding it to her does not release your liability to the mortgage company.

If she misses a payment, the company will pursue you for it. That means calls, collections letters and, possibly, a lawsuit.

Most guys, while fearful that this will happen, do nothing in their decree to protect themselves if it does.

You should require her to refinance the mortgage and provide you with proof of her attempts on a regular basis until she does so. Also include enforcement language to back it up so you will not be held liable.

I refuse to pay alimony.

Alimony is not all that bad – really. Many guys refuse to pay alimony because they think writing a check every month for years to an ex is tantamount to reliving the divorce every month.

However, alimony is tax deductible from income to you and taxable as income to your ex-wife. You should think of it as a tax planning measure.

If you have a choice of paying $5,000 a year as a "property settlement," which is not deductible to you, and $5,000 a year as spousal support, which is deductible, then go for it.

Just be sure the support amount is not modifiable upward; otherwise, your ex could reap the benefit of your pay raises post-divorce.

Make sure the payment you make in respect of Alimony is not considered as 'Voluntary Payment', by getting a court order. That is, there must be a court order or statement specifically mentioning in your Settlement Agreement that the amount paid is for Alimony, in-addition to filing tax return for the year separately, else the entire amount you paid will go down the drain as voluntary payment which in not tax-deductible.

She's begging for more financial support, so I'll give her a little now.

If you pay child support, you will get the sob story from your ex-wife: "I haven't received the check, I need extra money for clothes, etc."

It's tempting to make a direct payment, lest you leave a kid without food to eat and a bed to sleep on.

But this is a trap. Make a direct payment, and, in most jurisdictions, you will not receive a credit toward the child support you should have paid unless the paying parent keeps a copy of the payment (no cash, please!) and a receipt, and both parents agree the payment was intended to replace that support.

In many states, the direct payment is considered a gift – no ifs, ands or buts about it. That means you must pay the same support twice.

Many times in a divorce, one spouse will have to leave the house and live elsewhere while the case is pending. Sometimes that spouse will leave without taking furniture or personal items with the intention of getting them later. Unfortunately, more often than not, items left behind that you want will disappear. You can accuse the other spouse of throwing them away, but all he or she will have to say is, "I don't know what you're talking about. I don't have them."

Something else that can happen is the spouse claims that you gave her the item so she sold it. If there's no documentation of that, it's a he said/she said scenario and there's not much the judge or your attorney can do at this point. You have to offer proof that the items are in the possession of the other spouse or that you never agreed to give that item to your spouse. A great way to do that is to send your spouse an e-mail confirming what items there are and what you've agreed to take and if this is not the agreement, to respond and say so.

TIPS FOR MOVING OUT IN A DIVORCE

1. Make an inventory.

Go through the house and take pictures of everything in the house and make an inventory of everything there. You're going to need that for your attorney anyway. Most importantly, remove all important documents, treasured photographs and personal items and take them to your office or leave them with a friend for safekeeping. If you can't remove the documents, then make copies of them.

2. Secure your personal information.

Change your passwords for all your online accounts so your spouse can't go through them. Get a post office box and start having your mail sent there to keep your mail from disappearing.

3. Keep track of your credit.

If your spouse is paying certain bills that are in your name or both your names, stay on top them

and make sure they're being paid. It's a good idea
to subscribe to a credit reporting service that will
e-mail you every time there are changes to your
credit. If you find that your spouse quit paying
certain bills, you'll quickly know this so you can
take steps to minimize the damage.

4. Use your attorney to protect assets.
You can also utilize your attorney to make sure
that the marital assets are listed and protected
through injunctions. his way, neither party can
say they never received any e-mails regarding the
items as it's all done through the attorneys. You
can also have your attorney agree with your
spouse's attorney to file formal inventories of the
assets with the court. Usually, these inventories
don't include listing every piece of furniture, every
dish, or linen item, but you can agree to list those
things in addition to the major assets of the
estate.

"Blamers are not usually good at negotiation and other forms of compromise. They have all-or-nothing thinking, they personalize even the most minor issues, and they may feel that *giving in* to the other party's requests is a form of abandonment or threat to their superiority". This type of individual sees compromise as *losing* and people who are willing to accept a fair compromise as *losers*. "Borderlines feel that they must refuse compromise to avoid feeling abandoned. Narcissists feel that they are superior and should receive more." Although, I think in most cases both of these cognitive distortions are often at work.

This is also is why so many of them have a difficult time articulating what they want in terms of a settlement at the onset of the divorce process. She's reluctant to agree to anything because she wants to extract the maximum amount from you. *"If he's willing to give me this, maybe I can gouge another pound of flesh."* The actual monetary amount/degree of custody is meaningless; if she gets more, in her mind it means she wins and is right and will be viewed by others as the winner who's in the right.

"When you are negotiating with a Blamer, they will pressure you to give them much more than a court would give them because they were abandoned or are superior". Mediation and other collaborative techniques are difficult for severe Blamers because "they cannot handle compromises, they cannot listen to ideas that conflict with their reality.

The divorce process gives individuals like your wife a *raison d'être*. Women with these issues often have no interests (other than controlling you), identity or personal/career goals. Divorce and annihilating you becomes their new full-time job. Even after you both agree to a settlement, individuals like your wife will have their attorney try to revise and rewrite the terms in an effort to prolong the process and the attention she receives from it, to get more than her fair share, and to maintain her control over you by not letting you get on with your life. If you think about it, it's actually pretty pathetic. People who are in their right minds want to end this adversarial and emotionally and financially costly process as quickly as possible, *not* prolong it.

High-conflict people feed off of conflict and chaos. It gives them a buzz. For many, the only way they know how to relate to others is through aggression, blame and playing the victim. Once it ends, what does she have left? *Nothing.*

Oppositional withholding. This is more leftover baggage from your marriage. Many of these women are *withholding partners*. Meaning, if there's something you really want, she doesn't want you to have it. The more you want something, no matter how insignificant and small, the more she finds reasons that you shouldn't have it or actively obstructs you from getting it. In this respect, these women are like oppositional, defiant and absurd. The more you want to wrap up the divorce; the more she digs in her heels and tries to delay it.

The Endless Bag of Cluster B Tricks: Derailing and Tangenting.

Many of the men become stonewalled by their exes just as they near the finish line. These men are neither personality disordered nor high-conflict; they just want to be *done*. Every time they get close to a settlement, their ex derails, blows up or delays the process by not responding to letters, canceling appointments, making new

allegations and demands and/or walking out on settlement talks with mediators, evaluators, etc. This is a Cluster B trait that is appropriately called *derailing*.

In your case, **derailing is an attempt to intentionally try to destroy the progress you've made in your settlement talks**. For example, during negotiations, you're able to get through most of the issues calmly and reasonably. The process seems to be going well and you're hopeful that you'll be able to resolve the matter. Once you're close to an agreement, your ex jumps to a hot button topic (*e.g., having to support herself, your new girlfriend, your family whom she hates, accusations that you're hiding money—it could be anything*).

"The topic is usually one in which somehow something that you have done, are thinking of doing or [she] believes you have done or are thinking of doing. The rationality of the accusation, despite any information to the contrary, is irrelevant. Then [she] escalates that topic to its worst, going into a rage". This may end in her storming out of the session and reneging on items to which she previously agreed. This behavior destroys any progress that's been made and puts you back at square one.

Tangenting is a less explosive form of derailing, but with the same end result. For example, when you're just about to reach a solution, your ex will "change the subject, go sideways to a related, but different topic and refuse to return to the original issue. She may even project and blame you for obstructing the process, which is just another a side topic to keep you from returning to the original topic and its solution. These side topics are also never resolved.

"There is some logic to the connection between the topics that, on the surface, appears rational." This second topic is usually a recurring one that makes you the target of more blame. These make convenient side issues when a solution is too closely approached. When you attempt to bring the discussion back to the original topic, [she] will usually accuse you of being too controlling or that you think the world revolves around you". Both tangenting and derailing are often used to prolong the divorce process.

So What Can You Do?

Attorneys and mediators approximate that they accomplish 5 minutes of work for every hour spent with a high-conflict person. This is all well and good, but legal services aren't cheap and why should you get stuck footing the bill because your ex has issues?

1. Tell your attorneys what your bottom line is and stick to it. Let him or her communicate with your ex, since it doesn't seem that you're able to bring this to a conclusion with her. She is probably too stuck in the role of opposing and punishing you for you to make any headway with her.

2. Maximize any leverage you have. These women tend to be transactional in their relationships, so you might want to find something to withhold from her in order to get a more equitable outcome. Also, stop being so damned reasonable. Being fair and reasonable doesn't compute for this type of individual.

When you're generous and give away more than you're obligated, she sees it as a greenlight to push for even more. She doesn't think, *"Wow, he's being so generous. I'll take it."* She thinks, *"Sucker. I'll bet I can get even more if he's willing to agree to this."*

You are probably a very nice guy and want to be seen as a nice, reasonable guy. She knows this and is working you. The reality is that **no matter what you do, your ex thinks you're a jerk. When you're reasonable or make concessions to her demands, she thinks you're a *stupid jerk*.** No matter what you do, she's going to see you as the bad guy, so do what you need to do protect your best interests. High-conflict people/bullies only respect people who push back hard. Don't sink to her level, but it may be time to play hardball.

3. Choose your battles. Determine what's most important to you, but don't let her know. Remember, most of these types withhold to punish. Pretend like you don't care about the things you care about most and care about the things you don't really care about. This doesn't always work, but it's worth a shot.

4. Get it in writing. If you finally do reach a settlement via mediation or another process, *don't let her leave without signing something!* Don't give her time to think it over. Whenever possible, get commitments from her in writing right then and there. Verbal agreements from this kind of person are meaningless. Often, their written agreements are also meaningless since many Narcissists, Borderlines, Histrionics and other high-conflict types believe they're exempt from the rules by which the rest of us mere mortals abide. At least if you get something from her in writing you'll have some legal recourse if she later tries to obstruct or make new demands.

More and more spouses who are thinking about divorce, or who are going through the divorce process, are snooping on the other spouse. They're looking for evidence of adultery, hidden assets, bad parenting, or other information that might give them a leg up in a divorce or custody proceeding.

"Snooping" covers a wide range of activities. For instance, it could include accessing a spouse's private e-mail or social-networking account, looking in a spouse's smartphone for suspicious phone numbers or texts, or digging through his or her web search history.

Some spouses have been known to use methods that are more technologically sophisticated. These can include installing key-logging software on a computer that tracks every keystroke a spouse makes, setting up hidden cameras or recorders, attaching a GPS device to a spouse's car, or even swapping out a spouse's GPS device with a similar-looking device that transmits pictures of where the car goes and who's in the passenger seat.

SNOOPING ON YOUR SPOUSE MAY BE TEMPTING...BUT IT'S LEGALLY DANGEROUS

You might be tempted to snoop on a spouse or an ex-spouse, but if you are, it's absolutely critical to talk to a lawyer beforehand. This is because some of these practices could be illegal and get you arrested. In addition, the fact that you uncovered information illegally could cost you credibility in divorce court, and the evidence you came up with might not even be admissible in court if you obtained it through improper means.

If you discuss your concerns and suspicions with your attorney, your attorney may be able to use other methods to obtain the same kind of information without compromising your credibility or your case.

So what kinds of snooping are actually allowed?

It's perfectly legal to do a Google search on a spouse, for example. However, it's potentially illegal to hack into a spouse's password-protected smartphone or Facebook page. Although the law varies from place to place and situation to situation, this could constitute a serious violation of someone's electronic privacy rights.

Snooping on Your Spouse May Be Tempting...But It's Legally Dangerous

Installing a GPS device or key-logging software might also get you in trouble – especially if it's not clear that you have sole legal ownership of the car or the computer.

Hidden cameras and recording devices can create difficulties, too. They might violate wiretapping and other privacy laws.

For example, a man in California who was going through a bitter divorce discovered that his wife had sewn a tiny recording device into his son's blue jeans. Not only were he and his son recorded, but the device picked up conversations with lawyers, therapists, and members of the man's family. All these people have now filed lawsuits against the man's ex-wife, accusing her of violating federal laws against secret tape-recording.

In a similar case, a Nebraska woman who sewed a recording device into her four-year-old daughter's teddy bear now has to pay a significant damages award, plus attorney fees and costs, for violating her ex-husband's privacy.

SNOOPING ON YOUR SPOUSE MAY BE TEMPTING...BUT IT'S LEGALLY DANGEROUS

In the Omaha case, local media reports suggest the woman, Dianna Divingnzzo, used the teddy bear to conduct surveillance because it was her daughter's favorite toy. The bear's head was removed, the voice recorder implanted and the head reattached as part of the scheme, which was supposed to monitor visitations and provide information that would keep the child's father, William Duane Lewton, from obtaining additional custody rights. The child's father recently was granted partial custody.

Computer snooping can also get people into serious hot water. For example, a Michigan man accessed his estranged wife's e-mail on a shared computer and discovered that his wife – who'd been married twice before – was cheating on him with her second husband. He not only sought to use the information in his own divorce proceeding, but also printed out the e-mails and gave them to her first husband, with whom she was entangled in a custody dispute.

SNOOPING ON YOUR SPOUSE MAY BE TEMPTING...BUT IT'S LEGALLY DANGEROUS

The man – who claims he "guessed" the password to her Gmail account – was criminally charged and faces up to five years in prison.

If you're concerned about a spouse's improper financial, romantic or parenting activities, talk to your attorney. Don't just take the law into your own hands, or you might wind up on the wrong side of it.

What to do When Your Spouse is spying on you:

Some forms of spying aren't just offensive – they're illegal. Information a spouse uncovers about you via illegal spying can't be used against you directly in a divorce action or custody battle. However, if the illegally obtained information leads to legal sources of information, and your spouse can cover her tracks, then your spouse's spying could end up hurting you in court.

How can I tell if I'm being spied on?

Your spouse may be spying on you in any or all of a number of ways:

- Monitoring your mail, email, phone calls, and/or text messages
- Monitoring your use of social media (such as Facebook)
- Tracking you or your vehicle using GPS
- Having you "bugged"
- Watching you via video surveillance (including via a "nanny cam")
- Having you followed by a private investigator
- Following you personally

Keystroke logging (also called keylogging or keyboard capturing) software and hardware can allow your spouse to track every character you enter – including passwords to your personal financial accounts. There are tools (such as <u>this one</u>) you can use to detect whether there's a keystroke logger installed on your computer.

So how else can you tell if you have spyware on your computer?

An anti-virus program, such as McAfee or Norton, should be able to detect spyware (or prevent it from being installed in the first place). If you don't have anti-virus protection on your computer, you should get it for a lot of reasons – spying by your spouse is the least of your worries.

The Florida case of *O'Brien v. O'Brien* is illustrative. In this 2005 case, the husband and wife were seeking a divorce. Prior to a hearing, the wife had installed a certain spyware program onto her husband's computer. This particular program intercepted e-mails and electronic communications at the time they were either sent from or received by the husband's computer and then routed a copy of the intercepted message to a special file on the computer's hard drive. The wife would then access the secret file and retrieve the intercepted message.

Cell phone monitoring

Your spouse may be able to install a program like phonesheriff INVESTIGATOR that allows him or her to view your text messages, call history, GPS location, contacts, photos, and other information.   This particular program works by intercepting your iCloud backups, so if you change your iCloud password it will stop working.

If your Apple iPhone is "jailbroken," then it's especially vulnerable to spyware.

If YOU didn't jailbreak your phone, then your spouse may have done it in order to install spyware. Here's a site that will let you find out and restore the phone to the factory settings. Make sure your phone is backed up to iCloud before you reset it!

Landline monitoring and other bugs

Your spouse may have the expertise or resources to bug your home, office, car or (landline) phone. Here are some signs that you might have been bugged:

96

- You notice odd sounds or volume changes on your phone.
- You can hear sounds coming from your phone even after you hang up.
- Often when your phone rings there's nobody there, but you can hear a faint tone, squeal, and/or beep.
- Your TV or FM radio suddenly develops interference.
- Your electrical wall plates are out of place.
- You notice white-wall dust or debris on the floor.

Although it's sad to feel that you have to "look a gift horse in the mouth," a present from your spouse in the form of an electronic device (such as a clock radio, boom box, or CD player) or even a teddy bear may hide a bug or a surveillance device.

Being followed

How can you tell if you're being followed?

- Be aware of your surroundings. Don't always be staring at your cellphone or listening to music. Really notice the people you see and the cars that drive by.

- If you're driving, slow down, and notice if a car behind you slows down too. If you're on a highway, pull into the right lane and drive the speed limit (or just below it).

- If you're walking, stop suddenly. Have you phone set up to take a "selfie" and then use it to peak behind you and see if someone's waiting for you to start moving again.

Feuding couples are using spy technology, from phone tracking and GPS to hidden cameras and microphones, to secretly record their partner's movements. Some try to use the evidence in divorce court proceedings to get custody of children.

Brian, a father in Texas who asked that his last name not be used, said he made a shocking discovery on a recent visitation with his young son. Brian claimed his ex-wife, Allison, stitched a tiny tape recorder into their son's jeans and was using the boy to spy on him.

"My son told me, 'Dad, Mom has all these recordings of us inside the house.' I said, 'what do you mean?'" Brian said. "'She has all these recordings and she listens to them at night.' And I pulled my son close to me and patted him down,

and that's when I found the recorder."

Brian made a video recording of his own, showing what he said was documentation of the moment he found the recorder his wife had planted. His attorney has since filed a complaint in district court, alleging violation of wiretapping laws.

One of the primary reasons do-it-yourself snooping has become more widespread is because it is relatively cheap and easy. Surveillance equipment can cost less than $300, and spy gear that can't be found in a store can be bought online. Some recording devices are small enough to be mounted on a keychain, a motel room peephole, eyeglasses, pens or even inside a child's favorite toy.

"The one thing that's exchanged between the warring parties is the child, So the child becomes, in effect, some sort of Trojan horse." said John Kinney, a divorce attorney who has worked on a number of high-tech cases.

Duke Lewton has been on the other end of those devices in a vicious battle over his 7-year-old daughter, whose mother rigged her teddy bear with a microphone and told her to carry it at all times.

"[She] removed a few stitches, placed a recording device inside of the little bear's head, and then you could access a USB port on the side of the head ... and download all of our conversations that we had had through the weekend," Lewton told.

Failure to Evaluate Settlement Proposals will make you regret for life

If you're trying to decide whether your spouse's proposed divorce settlement is fair and workable, you should try to figure out how the settlement will impact your finances in the years ahead. There are many factors to consider, including assets, incomes, living expenses, inflation, alimony, child support, taxes, retirement plans, investments, medical expenses and health insurance costs, and child-related expenses such as education.

Do I Need an Attorney to Prepare the Divorce Agreement?

It's recommended that you hire a trustworthy lawyer (very difficult though) to prepare your Divorce Agreement. What you should do is, be clear about your legitimate rights and most importantly be aware about all possible traps that will make you penniless and suck your peace and haunt you for rest of the life. Never let your spouse's attorney draft the divorce agreement, remember your spouse's attorney will never consider your best interests or legitimate rights. It is your critical responsibility to protect your best interests. You should hire an attorney to review it (on your behalf) and make sure important legal provisions safeguarding your best interests are added, also make sure statements that bury your rights & best interests (that is traps), are deleted, and all your best interests are protected.

Phrases such as "sole legal custody," "exclusive possession," "timely indemnify and hold harmless," and "relinquish and waive all future claims" actually have very important meanings. You're not a lawyer, so you may miss serious problems with the proposed agreement, or may not know what specific words must be included to protect your interests. If you fail to catch something, you may end up losing important rights. The smart thing to do is to pay someone in the beginning to make sure you don't pay even more in the end.

After drafting of divorce agreement is done, ask second opinion from another lawyer whose office is at a different county/location which is far away from that of your spouse's lawyer. That is, one who is not a friend of your spouse lawyer and doesn't have the opportunity to have frequent acquaintance with your spouse's lawyer. Though it involves some cost, think it as a vital investment for rest of your life. There is a critical reason for saying this is, terms in divorce agreement will be binding on you for the rest of your life. Each and every word is critical. You need to make sure it is unambiguous without any traps, and that statements in it cannot be interpreted in any malicious way than what you intended to be its meaning. Once agreed and signed, you are bound to abide by the clauses mentioned in it.

If I like My Spouse's Proposed Divorce Agreement, Should I Just Sign it?

No. Even if you are completely ready to move forward with a settlement, if your spouse's attorney prepared the first draft, it's vital that you at least have the agreement scrutinized word by word by your own attorney – someone who's working to protect *your* interests. You should do this no matter how much pressure is put on you to sign and no matter how much you want to "keep it simple" without "getting all the lawyers involved."

It's important to remember that your spouse's attorney does not represent you and doesn't care whether the agreement is fair or provides you with adequate financial resources.

What if I Don't Like My Spouse's Proposed Divorce Agreement?

Don't sign it. Remember, it's just a proposal – a starting point in the negotiation. Even if your spouse (or your spouse's attorney) gave you a deadline to respond, you still don't have to do anything. You can throw the proposal in the trash if you want to. No one can force you to settle until you're ready.

But there is such a thing as waiting too long. If you refuse to negotiate in good faith, or you won't sign anything because you want to keep milking your spouse's generosity for as long as possible, your spouse will become frustrated, and may pull out of the settlement negotiations altogether. If you really want to settle, you need to be willing to move forward and compromise.

As stated above, it's wise to ask an attorney to thoroughly review your spouse's proposed Divorce Agreement word by word.

Discovery is typically a large part of litigation associates' respective workloads. A majority of case strategy is evaluating what discovery should be conducted and when. For example, seeking out third-party discovery early in a case may be strategically beneficial because information may be obtained that can be used later against opposing parties. Therefore, early evaluation of which third parties may provide useful information, as well as how that information will best be conveyed (e.g., documents, testimony, or both), usually will prove fruitful for the case and demonstrate initiative and critical thinking to a supervising attorney.

Identify the Proper Method of Service

Improper service is an easy way for a witness to object and delay the process; therefore, careful attention to effectuating proper service is important. Rule 45(b)(1) provides that "[a]ny person who is at least 18 years old and not a party may serve a subpoena. Serving a subpoena requires delivering a copy to the named person."

Although a majority of courts require personal service under Rule 45, some courts permit service by certified mail. ("The majority of courts hold that Rule 45 requires personal service. . . . The growing number of cases that have determined that Rule 45 does not require personal service have permitted service by certified mail and other means if the method of service is made in a manner designed to reasonably insure actual receipt of the subpoena.") Employing a method of service other than personal, however, should "reasonably insure actual receipt of [the] subpoena by the witness." As discussed below, preliminary communications with the witness may be helpful, because the witness may agree to accept service by mail. Any agreement relating to alternative service should be documented.

Consider Communicating with the Witness Prior to Issuing the Subpoena

It may be beneficial to contact the witness prior to issuing the subpoena. Third parties generally have no real stake in the outcome of the underlying litigation; therefore, making their lives easier, and compliance with the subpoena less cumbersome, may make the process less adversarial. For example, several potential issues may be negotiated prior to issuance of the subpoena. First, it may be beneficial to allow the recipient of the subpoena to suggest a reasonable compliance deadline or dates on which to schedule a deposition. Second, consider whether to offer to pay for or negotiate the costs of copying the requested documents. Third, determine whether the recipient is willing to accept an alternative method of service (e.g., certified mail or regular mail). Finally, be willing to negotiate the scope of the requested material or stipulate to a protective order, particularly if the information sought will implicate proprietary or trade secret material. Not only may the recipient appreciate your flexibility and accommodations, but also potential objections to the subpoena may be avoided. Individuals are also usually thankful to have someone explain to them that a process server will be delivering documents to them personally, an experience that may be unsettling or make the witness feel as though he or she has done something wrong. In addition, the specific timing and location of service can be agreed upon. It is important, however, to explain to the witness that you do not represent him or her.

Preparing a Subpoena Duces Tecum

A subpoena commanding the production of documents is often referred to as a subpoena duces tecum. Although preparation of a subpoena duces tecum is similar to preparing a request for the production of documents to an opposing party, be careful to tailor the requests appropriately. <u>Often, attorneys are fearful of missing something, meaning requests for documents are drafted more broadly than necessary.</u> Courts generally weigh a recipient's third-party status in favor of upholding objections based on over-breadth or undue burden. Anticipate such objections and draft the requests appropriately to avoid, or reduce the likelihood of success on, such objections. Like document requests served on a party, subpoenas duces tecum directed to third parties should include appropriate definitions and instructions. Beyond the general definitions and instructions typically included—such as "writing," party names, relevant abbreviations, relevant time period(s), and instructions relating to necessary privilege logs—it is also important to include definitions and instructions relating to electronically stored information (ESI). In particular, Rule 45(a)(1)(C) provides that a subpoena may specify "the form or forms in which electronically stored information is to be produced." If the subpoena does not specify the form, then Rule 45(d)(1)(B) provides that the individual or entity responding may produce all ESI in the manner "in which it is ordinarily maintained." Finally, do not forget to attach as exhibits all applicable protective orders active in the underlying litigation, as well as a copy of the operative complaint. These documents will further educate recipients on the underlying litigation, as well as guide them in preparing their response.

Third-party discovery provides ample opportunities to further build a case; however, sufficient preparation and attention to detail is necessary to successfully subpoena a witness or documents. The following checklist will serve as a good reminder:

1. Identify third-party witnesses and objectives of discovery (e.g., documents, testimony, or both).

2. Review applicable rules (e.g., Rule 45, local rules).

3. Identify appropriate jurisdiction from which the subpoena must issue.

4. Consider communicating with the witness prior to service of the subpoena.

5. Identify method of service (e.g., personal or certified mail).

6. Identify applicable fees.

7. Prepare requests for documents.

8. Prepare notice to parties.

9. Effectuate service of notice and subpoena.

10. File the notice of service, or proof of service, if required by local rules.

Commonly cited objections to Subpoena include

(1) Privileged or confidential

(2) Irrelevant

(3) Vague, ambiguous, or overbroad

(4) Undue burden.

Along with these possible objections, evaluate whether any requests are vague, ambiguous, or overbroad. Courts that have upheld objections based on over-breadth have sometimes predicated the ruling based on language such as "and all documents relating thereto." Requests that create any undue burden on the recipient also are objectionable.

Court may evaluate several factors when considering whether the subpoena creates an undue burden on the recipient, including non-party status, whether the discovery is "unreasonably cumulative or duplicative," whether the discovery sought is "obtain[able] from some other source that is more convenient, less burdensome, or less expensive," and whether the cost of the discovery outweighs its benefit.

Obtaining an appropriate award of spousal maintenance (alimony) or child support depends in large part on obtaining accurate information about your spouse's income. Many people believe that their spouses are hiding income. There are ways to determine income, or to make an educated guess about income that the court will consider in determining alimony or child support.

If you believe there is hidden income, there are several ways to determine actual income.

- **First, if possible, before you separate and litigation begins, make copies of all relevant financial documents you can obtain in your home, or if you have legal right to access them, in your spouse's place of business. These include financial statements from banks, credit unions, investment firms, or other financial institutions. You should also copy credit card statements, insurance policies, deeds and wills and trusts. The documents should be copied and returned to their original place. In this way, you will have sufficient account information to obtain further**

records, as well as any information about purchases and any estate planning that your spouse has engaged in. In addition, internal financial information such as ledgers, profit and loss statements, and income statements either in hard copy or on file on the computer should also be copied or downloaded for future reference–again, if you have legal right to access those records.

- Gather evidence of your standard of living during the marriage by cataloging expensive purchases and vacations. Take pictures of expensive items purchased during the marriage, and make copies of any appraisals or invoices showing the value of any personal property purchased.

- If you are leaving the marital home and your spouse is going to retain possession, take pictures of every room in the house to show the assets that are located there. This also helps when you are trying to negotiate for a division of the personal property.

- Obtain historic bank statements and bank loan files from any joint account. If you have a joint account with your spouse, the bank will provide you with back statements and cancelled checks and deposit slips. You may also be an officer in your spouse's business, and thus be able to request account information regarding your spouse's business. (You may be able to obtain information about your status in your spouse's business by going to the Secretary of State's website.)

- Check with your accountant or bookkeeper to see if he or she will provide you with financial documents. If the accountant worked for both you and your spouse, the accountant should provide you with any information concerning joint financial transactions–of, if you are an officer in your spouse's business, obtain financial information about the business.

- **Check and print all relevant information on social networking sites such as Facebook or Linkedin, which may show lifestyle**

information, asset purchases, or other financial information that your spouse may brag about. Be sure to do this as early as possible, before your spouse blocks the sites.

Once you obtain all the financial documents you can on your own, and litigation has started, your attorney should take the following steps:

- **Review your spouse's financial affidavits that are required to be filed with the court. These often reveal more than they intend to, including account information, household expenses, as well as lists and values of assets which may indicate higher income than your spouse has reported.**

- **File discovery requests asking for financial information that you were not able to obtain prior to litigation, such as names of financial institutions where your spouse has accounts. The opposing party is required to respond, and you will be surprised how much information you can**

**glean from the responses even if your
spouse is hiding income.**

- If bank accounts are in your spouse's name
  alone, or he or she has separate business
  bank accounts, your attorney can subpoena
  bank records. The law requires that a bank
  must notify the account holder of the
  subpoena, and if the account holder
  objects, you will be required to go to court
  to obtain an order for production. However,
  the information is relevant in a divorce
  case, and the court in most cases will order
  the bank comply with your request. You will
  have to pay the cost of production, but the
  cost has come down substantially because
  of the new technologies the banks now
  use to store information. You should ask the
  bank for statements, check images, deposit
  slips and deposited items. If your spouse
  has only one account, then it is easy to
  determine how much income your spouse is
  actually collecting if he or she is depositing
  income into bank accounts. Determining
  actual income is more difficult when there
  is more than one account, and funds are

117

transferred between accounts. You will have to try to follow the funds through each of the accounts, and you may need a forensic accountant or other financial

expert to sift through the accounts. If there are multiple accounts, cancelled checks and deposited items can help follow the money trail.

- **Subpoena your spouse's bank loan files. They are revealing, because when people want a bank loan, they want to demonstrate that they have the means to repay, so their financial statements filed with the bank often look entirely different than the income tax return filed with the IRS. The bank loan files also should include the bank's analysis of the application and other financial information and notes. Therefore, when you subpoena the bank loan files, you should ask for the entire file.**

- Subpoena your spouse's bookkeeper or accountant to a deposition, and request that person to bring your spouse's files. You can also require your spouse to testify under oath at a deposition. At a deposition, it is sometimes easier to force a deponent to provide information about financial accounts and records than requesting that information through written interrogatories and requests to produce.

- Have a forensic accountant or your attorney's financial consultant review financial records of your spouse's business to determine whether the expenses of the business include any personal expenses. If they do, those personal expenses will be considered by the court to be personal income.

- Other sources showing life style or income are UCC filings, obtainable online, which will reveal personal property purchases that your spouse took out a loan on; Dun and Bradstreet reports, and department of motor vehicle records.

There are traditionally three ways through which child support is paid to a receiving parent. These three methods include payments made: (1) through direct payment by the paying parent to the receiving parent; (2) through the Family Support Payment Center; or, (3) through a wage withholding on the paying parent's paychecks. Parents can choose which option works best for them, although seeking the opinion of an experienced family law attorney is always recommended so that the particular circumstances of your situation are factored into this decision-making process.

(1) Child Support Payments Made Directly from One Parent to Another

Parents receiving child support often choose to receive payments directly from the paying parent. Often, this option is chosen because receiving parents believe it is easier than the other options and that they'll get their money faster if they take it directly from the paying parent. Paying parents also like the simplicity of this option in that they are in charge of when and how the child support is made, whether it be by cash, check or direct deposit into the receiving parent's bank account. Unfortunately, one of the negative aspects of this method is often it is difficult for parties to prove that payments were or weren't made, particularly if they were made in cash. Thus, if the case is brought back to court at a later date, it is hard for a Judge to see which payments were made and if the payment made was actually for child support or for another expense, such as daycare or medical co-pay reimbursement.

(2) Child Support Payments Made Through the Family Support Payment Center

Through this option, payments are made by the paying parent to the Family Support Payment Center in the state. Acting as a trustee, the Family Support Payment Center accepts this money on behalf of the receiving parent and then makes a payment to the receiving parent on behalf of the paying parent. This option is ideal for those people that want to make sure every single payment is tracked by the State, particularly if they need to later bring a case of contempt for nonpayment of child support. It also allows both parties to keep track online of the payments made. One drawback of this payment method is that there can often be a delay in receiving the payments from the Family Support Payment

121

Center, especially for the first month's payment, which some parents find frustrating.

3) Child Support Payments Made Through a Wage Withholding:

A wage withholding is another method by which child support payments can be executed. A wage withholding is filed with the Family Court and then sent to the employer of the paying parent. The employer must then follow certain guidelines, and deduct a portion of the paying parent's wages each month. That money is then sent to the receiving parent.

Low- and moderate-income families may qualify for one or more of four federal tax credits — the Child Tax Credit, the Additional Child Tax Credit, the Earned Income Tax Credit and the Child and Dependent Care Credit. The credits' rules overlap in some ways and differ in others, but many families may qualify for all four.

1) Child Tax Credit

The Child Tax Credit is a federal tax credit worth up to $1,000 per child in tax year 2011. Families must have dependent children under age 17 to get it. Millions of families became eligible last year even if they owed no taxes. The additional tax credit comes as a refund from the IRS to families making more than $3,000 in 2011.

The Child Tax Credit first reduces or eliminates a family's income tax bill of $1,000 or less. Any portion that remains comes back as a refund for families making more than $3,000 in the form of the Additional Child Tax Credit (see below). The total size of the additional credit depends on the amount by which the family's earned income exceeds $3,000, and the credit is phased out for families with adjusted gross incomes above:

- $110,000 if married filing jointly;

- $75,000 if single, head of household, or qualifying widow(er);
- $55,000 if married filing separately.

2) Additional Child Tax Credit

The Additional Child Tax Credit is available even if someone does not make enough money to claim the entire $1,000 Child Tax Credit. Unlike the nonrefundable Child Tax Credit portion, the refundable Additional Child Tax Credit comes in the form of a refund even if you do not still owe taxes. The size of the Additional Child Tax Credit depends on how much the family income exceeds $3,000 and is subject to the same income phase out limits as the Child Tax Credit.

3) Earned Income Tax Credit

The Earned Income Tax Credit is a special tax benefit for low- to moderate-income workers. It reduces their tax burden, supplements wages and makes work more attractive than public benefits. The credit can mean up to $3,094 for workers raising one child in their home, up to $5,112 for workers raising more than two children, or up to $5,751 for workers raising three or more children.

Although children must meet residency requirements, a child does not have to be claimed as a dependent to qualify a worker for the Earned Income Tax Credit. Even workers without children can qualify for up to $464.

The Earned Income Tax Credit is for full-time or part-time, single or married workers raising at least one qualifying child at home — and for some childless workers. Workers must meet certain income standards. A qualifying child is a son, daughter, stepchild, adopted child, agency-placed foster child or grandchild, or a sibling, stepsibling, niece, nephew, stepniece or stepnephew being raised as the taxpayer's own. Any qualifying child must be under age 19, under 24 if in school full-time for at least five months during 2011, or any age if totally disabled.

4) Child and Dependent Care Credit

The Child and Dependent Care Credit is a tax benefit that helps families pay for child care while they work or look for work. It also helps workers pay for the care of a spouse or adult dependent, who is incapable of self-care. It can offset taxes taken out as payroll withholding and cover what is still owed at the end of the year, depending on the size of the credit. In most cases, the credit can only be claimed for a child who is claimed as a dependent, but there are special rules for children of divorced or separated parents.

The Child and Dependent Care Credit differs from both the Earned Income Tax Credit and the Child Tax Credit in that families earning too little to pay federal income tax cannot take the Child and Dependent Care Credit. The Child and Dependent Care Credit are between 20 and 35 percent of expenses up to $3,000 for one child or dependent or up to $6,000 for more than one child or dependent. It can mean a credit up to $1,050 for families with one child or dependent in care, or up to $2,100 for families with more than one child in care.

Importance of Filing Correctly

Before we get into the hows and whys of single and head of household status, I want to mention three key points:

- **Keep Your W-4 Up to Date.** If you are a newly single parent, according to the IRS, you must submit an updated W-4 form with your employer within ten days of your divorce being finalized. This will help keep your federal income tax withholding accurate.

- **Your Status Carries Over.** Your legal, marital status on the last day of any tax year will basically determine your filing status for that entire year. If you were divorced on December 31 of last year, then you are considered divorced for the entire year in the eyes of the IRS.

- **You Don't Want to Screw This Up.** Believe me, even though you may consider yourself

127

to be the "head of the household," you may not be under the rules of the IRS. Make sure you do your research and get it right the first time. It's not like you can file your taxes with an incorrect status and wonder if the IRS will ever figure it out. By filing under an incorrect status, you risk having your entire return rejected by the IRS, or being subject to additional taxes, interest, and penalties.

Basically, while filing incorrectly could help you out in the immediate future, if it's done wrong, it could become costly over the long run. Keep these points in mind as you read on.

Filing as Single – Qualifications

As far as figuring out if you qualify as a "single" person, the guidelines are pretty straightforward. According to the IRS, your filing status is single if, on the last day of the year, you are unmarried or legally separated from your spouse under a divorce or separate maintenance decree, *and you do not qualify for another filing status.*

But, if you do have to file as single, there is a silver lining:

- **Simplified Returns.** Your return should be much easier to compile. You might even be able to use the 1040-EZ form rather than the standard 1040 tax form. This means you could utilize free online tax preparation software and services.

- **Less Paperwork to Dig For.** Additionally, you can look forward to a less complex return as you are only filing your taxes based upon your own personal tax documents. This means less research and less document gathering. Trust me, this could be a big benefit if you are recently divorced and are not on the greatest terms with your ex-spouse.

Filing as Head of Household – Qualifications

The rules for being eligible for head of household are complicated, extensive, and very specific. In fact, they are so specific that I am not able to outline every single qualifier in this article. I strongly encourage you to talk to your accountant or visit the IRS website before determining your filing status.

In a nutshell, here are the qualifications:

1. Dependents

You must have a qualifying dependent who is related to you and also meets the requirements to be either a "qualifying child" or "qualifying relative."

- **Qualifying Relative.** In order to be considered a qualifying relative, that person must not meet the requirements as a qualifying child or relative of anyone else. Their gross income must be less than your federal exemption amount for that year, and you must have had provided more than half the support of that person during the calendar year.

- **Qualifying Child.** The person must be under 19 years of age, or a full-time student under the age of 24. They must have lived with you for more than half the year and not have provided for more than half of his or her own support.

2. Housing Costs

You must also pay more than half the costs for the maintenance of the home in which you and your qualifying dependent lived for more than half the year.

To illustrate a little more clearly, a person found that he qualified for the head of household status because he was divorced late last year and therefore paid for more than half the support of his son (my qualifying child) for the calendar year. His son did not meet the requirements as a qualifying child for anyone else, and also lived with him for more than half the year.

If the parents do not file a joint return together but both parents claim the child as a qualifying child, the IRS will treat the child as the qualifying

child of the parent with whom the child lived for the longer period of time in a year. If the child

lived with each parent for the same amount of time, the IRS will treat the child as the qualifying child of the parent who had the higher adjusted gross income (AGI).

In very limited instances, you may qualify to file as head of household even if you are still legally married.

Benefits

In short, although it may be much more difficult to decipher whether or not you qualify for head of household, if you do, the tax breaks are significant. Here are a couple of ways you'll benefit:

1. **Higher Standard Deduction.** The standard deduction for head of household is much higher ($8,500 for head of household vs. $5,800 for single filers).

2. **More Favorable Tax Rates.** You get more favorable tax rates because, as a head of household filer, you qualify for lower tax brackets (depending on your income) than you would if you filed single.

Ultimately, with these benefits, it is clear that filing as head of household is a much better option than filing as single.

Be sure to investigate the matter thoroughly. If you do qualify for head of household status, then file that way! Your benefits are sure to be worth the effort.

Important IRS links:

http://www.irs.gov/publications/p503/ar02.html

http://www.irs.gov/publications/p504/ar02.html

http://www.irs.gov/Help-&-Resources/Tools-&-FAQs/FAQs-for-Individuals/Frequently-Asked-Tax-Questions-&-Answers/Filing-Requirements,-Status,-Dependents,-Exemptions/Dependents-&-Exemptions/Dependents-&-Exemptions-7

http://www.irs.gov/uac/Interactive-Tax-Assistant-%28ITA%29-1

http://www.irs.gov/uac/Am-I-Eligible-for-the-Child-Tax-Credit%3F

http://www.irs.gov/pub/irs-pdf/p501.pdf

http://www.irs.gov/individuals/qualifying-child-of-more-than-one-person

Alimony Paid (Official IRS Rules):

Amounts paid under divorce or separate maintenance decrees or written separation agreements entered into between you and your spouse or former spouse will be considered alimony for federal tax purposes if:

- You and your spouse or former spouse do not file a joint return with each other

- You pay in cash (including checks or money orders)

- The payment is received by (or on behalf of) your spouse or former spouse

- The divorce or separate maintenance decree or written separation agreement does not say that the payment is not alimony

- If legally separated under a decree of divorce or separate maintenance, you and your former spouse are not members of the same household when you make the payment

- You have no liability to make the payment (in cash or property) after the death of your spouse or former spouse, and

- Your payment is not treated as child support or a property settlement

www.ingramcontent.com/pod-product-compliance
Lightning Source LLC
Chambersburg PA
CBHW051922170526
45168CB00001B/496